Manna

Cristina Cobos Tapia

UNIVERSO de LETRAS

Manna
Cristina Cobos Tapia

© Cristina Cobos Tapia, 2024

Diseño de la cubierta:
    Equipo de diseño de Universo de Letras
Imagen de cubierta:
    ©Shutterstock.com

Obra publicada por el sello Universo de Letras
universodeletras.com

Primera edición: 2024

ISBN: 9788410003965
ISBN eBook: 9788410005785

1

There is no way, we living this nightmare, while most people do not want to know anything about anything, 'they know,' 'they sense,' but they close their eyes with what intention? They are afraid that it is real so much evil? so much aberration? It is normal to have that reaction. It is completely normal to look the other way. But we cannot afford to evade reality, and... that makes me nervous...! impotence? pain? despair?...

Almost three years have passed, where the lie, (the big lie) was and continues to 'roam' at ease while people died and die non-stop. Everyone went out to applaud every day on their balconies, because that is how the advertising of the great television had ordered it.

Meanwhile..., from my balcony, I observed people, I felt, I noticed..., that something was wrong while I was clapping..., and I went back home, to the prison where they had locked us up for our sake. A good for everyone that never came, a good for us that suffocated us with so many rules, which worked perfectly to kill.

Who should die first? The weakest, how weak? people with depression, with an addiction, how were they going to die? simple. They would eliminate themselves.

Yes, thousands of people committed suicide in this country, and, in all countries of the world, the result of good social engineering. No soldiers were needed for such an atrocity, psychologists and sociologists were used. My little brother died at the age of forty-five, the result of their 'fair rules,' which they created for our good. They had no qualms about recording his death, putting up the fashionable disease sign. Yes, all the people who died were given the same label, and thus they got people terrified of such misfortune. The televisions filled people with fear day and night on all channels because that is what they were and 'are' destined for. The television and the official written press belonged and belongs today to those tolerant tyrants who 'fight' for our good, the official journalists, cackle incessantly, that the elderly infect others, and they die devoured by fear. Most of them are separated from their families, isolated and terrified, believing that they were the responsible because the television said so. Although soon the soldiers of the information, began to vomit at all hours, that the carriers of such a cruel disease, were the children, yes, 'our' children.

Our little ones were the 'danger,' a danger that would make their grandparents sick and kill them, and that could not be tolerated!

We had to save the grandparents, and they put a toll, so that the grandparents could see their grandchildren, and another toll, so that the children could see their grandparents. Plastic barriers to be hugged, gloves and masks, but what luck! we could use the screens! and thus be able to have a virtual face! All separated and divided, but very grateful because our rulers gave us the guidelines to follow to take any step, anything we had to do or say, 'if' they also told us what we had to say, what we had to talk to, and with whom, and for that they had their soldiers, the 'journalists,' to give us instructions to talk and above all 'not to talk.'

2

Not talking, is also part of the plan, and for our sake they put the mask in our mouth, according to them, to save us from such misfortune that plagued the entire world. Nor could we approach a meter and a half between person and person, separated from each other, without being able to speak, and that protected our enemy. An enemy who does not want us to communicate, because he is in danger of being discovered. And in this way the clashes between the people began. If a person wore the mask under their nose, or simply did not wear it, the same citizens would scold and insult them for fear of catching it. Madness! was settling in, managed by our caretakers, the Rulers.

Yes, our 'rulers,' raising money with full hands! they get rich from our health, they lock us up for our health, they pay their television soldiers to spit fear continuously for our health, they raise taxes for our health, what more can we ask for? Being healthy was the most important thing! Not having the damn disease was the project of all the institutions in the world! or *Munda*! Because in the midst of so much world chaos, a minister from Spain, had a great idea that was going to help us get out of our problems, the world would no longer be called the world!, it would be called *Munda*!, yes, as you are hearing it, suddenly the words that had always been written and heard and masculine, began to be recited in feminine! One day I heard our handsome and brand-new president, saying in the congress of deputies, (members and members), but worst of all, is that people repeat, like parrots to which robots.

Another completely stupid and useless change, has been the inclusive language, totally embarrassing to listen to, in a meeting, rally, conversation and even posters everywhere, them and them, you and you, and so tired and sickly, with anything that was talked about. But again, most people, I would repeat and repeat all this ridiculous nonsense. Everything has an end, and that is, 'indoctrinating,' manipulating even with nonsense. They had to know, that they could manipulate the mass, to carry out their plan.

Plan?, for what?, what plan do they have or did they have for us?..., they already manipulate us, we already pay everything they want, we also comply with all the new norms and rules, that they have imposed on us, that they want to want more from us?, we are exemplary citizens, but what we do not know about us, is that we are the 'mass.' A mass that must disappear because someone has decided so.

Finally came the solution to the great disease, which they had (imposed) on us. The 'vaccine,' in a few months, they already had their miraculous potion, the manna that terrified people eagerly awaited! To be able to continue with their lives! the same lives they led before so much pandemic misfortune.

The television soldiers are preparing the ammunition to be fired, the 'target,' the population. A population that does not expect such aberration, betrayal, and that yearns, most of them, to be rescued with such a miraculous potion. The great presentation of the vaccine has arrived, on the news!, excited!, hopeful!, my God!, what luck we have had!, we will all return to our lives as before!, the soldiers of television, have delivered the head of all the citizens of the country, on a silver platter, to their executioners.

They were already preparing at full speed, the crime scenes, which were called, 'vaccinator.'

3

The official media began to sell the long-awaited vaccine, in all their programs and chains without rest. They used the tricks and traps they wanted, to push people to inoculate themselves. But the creepiest, and disgusting, was the discovery of the 'experts,' some characters who one day had an opinion, and a few days later said the opposite, depending on the amount of money they had received. People flocked to inoculate the brew, hopeful and excited, and what became fashionable? because fashion is to upload images of them on social networks, while they poked them smiling, such a blessed potion. They walked down the street proudly with their band-aid on their arms, because that meant that they had behaved well. Yes, the little soldiers on TV, tattled at all hours, of the great action of vaccinating themselves for the common good, the 'experts' blew to which trumpet, which inoculating themselves with such a substance, is an act of solidarity. If you get vaccinated, you are protecting others! Pure marketing! super promotion of the experimental miracle drug, which is what we saw as exhausted spectators, a small part of the population.

Well, no, not everyone saw it as something positive, everything that happened, on the contrary, we saw the bad disguised as medicine. Of course! they knew that a small group of people were going to realize the 'lie,' and they already had the name prepared, what name? Deniers and anti-vaccines. All the people who inoculate themselves are classified as 'heroes,' and that made increased people go to the ranks of illness and death. Not in the worst fiction films, would we have imagined something so terrifying. What would we do? would we tell people? we warned them? but how? in what way? The blind faith to television, had people, totally abducted and educated , what could we do?, we had to warn them that those syringes, were not to prevent any infection, but how were they going to believe us?..., at home I said the same day that they presented the 'vaccine,' that we would never puncture ourselves.

I alerted a mom at school, with whom I used to go to the park with our kids, not to inject herself, but it did not help. To the people I saw in parks I also informed them without any success, I felt inside me, despair! a suffering! but everything was in vain. Shortly after starting their 'vaccination' plan, they began asking for children in a hospital to, according to them, experiment, I was terrified, everything was getting worse inside me. Not only were they going after us, but they were also going after our children.

I was losing mental strength, I felt dejected and anguished, because I did not know how I was going to protect my nine-year-old son. I did not want him to go to school! In my mind, I imagined, that he was pricked without my consent, and I could not get it out of my head. In the macabre agenda of tyrants, they have no place, children with disabilities, my son is autistic and attends a special school three days a week, and Thursday and Friday, he studies in a normal school. That is, to monitor the two schools, in case they plotted to poke on them. All those thoughts weakened me, fortunately it did not happen, but they did poke treacherously in other schools in the country. The media prostitutes went to all lengths, regarding the injectable, accusing the unspoked of being unsupportive people for not wanting the fashionable disease to disappear. The slimy talkies, and one presenter after another, asked that such evil denialist and anti-vaccine people be labeled with a sticker on their clothes, in the most Nazi style. They asked that they not be allowed to leave the house, nor enter the establishments, and even that they not be treated in hospitals. We were insulted, humiliated, and even treated as murderers! A famous Spanish biologist, reported on his social networks that the complete pattern would never exist, since the intention of the authorities is to inject their potion, throughout life.

4

Yes, all my life poking, it is the intention of the authorities, they plan to do it to the entire population, but that, only the deniers knew. The only people who began to investigate, and to be interested in what was inside the injectable. They also went to great lengths to find out, who or who had organized, this entire world terror plan.

Ricardo Delgado, a Spanish biostatistician, began to investigate what they were injecting into people, and got four vials of assorted brands into his hands. He suspected that the vials contain a very dangerous material for humans. Inoculated people began to appear, with magnetism in their arms, that is, after the inoculation, many people appeared on social networks, with cutlery magnetized on their arms and chest. The magnetization is so exaggerated, that even the mobile phone remained stuck in the area that had been injected. Ricardo suspected that the toxicant could be graphene oxide, a material that, together with a cell, becomes magnetic. For that he sent the vials to Doctor Campra, a scientist also Spanish, who had the courage to analyze the vials and 'bingo,' Campra found graphene oxide, in all the vials. Ricardo wanted and wants to tell the world what happens with vaccines, and so began his fight, which was clearly followed by other scientists in the world. Graphene oxide with its magnetic phenomenon, inside the human body, coagulates the blood, which is why many people have thrombi, strokes, arrhythmias, etcetera, graphene oxide also works with micro–outbreaks, that is, as the material is modulable, when irradiating it looks for the electrical organs, the heart, and the brain. Ricardo together with his great friend the Sevillian Doctor, are up to date today, with their fight for the justice of human beings, without any benefit and risking their lives every day.

While the prostitutes of the system inform us every week of a new variant of the disease, every week a new variant came. What variant? If the government has said that they do not have the virus isolated or purified, and that they do not know which country has it. So where do the variants come from? the stick they use to detect such an evil disease, which has killed millions of people in the world, was used for all the variants! The famous PCR that was invented by Kary Mullis, was not used to detect any infection. Kary Mullis died in strange circumstances, a few months before starting the global genocidal plan, coincidence? or causality? When they needed a new 'outbreak,' they tested the stick, which even tested positive in the water. Let us not forget that mucus is made up of 90% water, if I am interested in creating a new 'outbreak,' I just have to do that fraudulent test, to all the people I want, and I can already lock them up and manipulate them at will, and thus I will scare others, because the deadly virus can kill them at any time. So, that for which do people die? What happened to the elderly who lived in the residences? Let us not forget that only the elderly of the residences died, because those who were in their homes were fine, what happened? They were locked up ten days before the pandemic began, abandoned, and confined to their rooms, alone. Most died because they were given morphine. The population must have been terrified, but for this, they needed them, and not exactly alive.

But there are too many collaborators wrapping the official version, without a doubt, the most dangerous have been the official media, which have manipulated, terrorized, and pushed the population, including children, to illness and death. They have the entire system, justice, health, they have absolutely everything, to commit the greatest genocide in the entire history of humanity.

5

And what do those of us who refuse to follow the political game do? because they also invented their political passport! of course! the 'green pass' is the prize you get if you poke yourself with its wonderful poison! They would not let you travel if you did not have the mark of the beast..., for months the unvaccinated were forbidden to enter, in hospitality establishments, while thousands of people poke themselves just to travel, or enter a bar. Many people go to bed and wake up dead in their bed. They begin to die in the planes, finding corpses in the seats, even the pilots also die in mid-flight, because they were forced to inoculate themselves. But no one suspected anything, no one linked the deaths to the 'vaccine,' and in the official media, 'No' reports on these deaths. The orders that the media bloodsuckers receive are; 'hide the truth.' Television bloodsuckers also get sick and die from the vaccine, but even they do not suspect that it is because of the magic potion.

The 'lethal' antivaccine are beginning to investigate who is behind so much barbarism! It is a group of very rich families, who have held the reins of the entire world for decades. They had been planning their genocidal plan for many years. 'The 2030 agenda,' which they had disguised as good intentions. They intend to reduce the world's population by less than half, they want to get rid of about five billion people, and even more, 70% of the world's population, is already injected with graphene oxide and nanotechnology. But we do not know the life expectancy of people who are still alive. Because a lot of people have died, including children. Hospitals are full of people with blood clots, strokes, heart attacks and all kinds of cardiovascular diseases, in pediatrics the stroke code has been activated for more than a year, children and young people with heart attacks, myocarditis, pericarditis, the soldiers of television, have managed to make their 'contract work' works. Turning to these wealthy families who have all the governments bought off, they are nothing less than the owners of WHO, UNICEF and all the charitable organizations, which only want the common good, for all the people of the world. Who dictates such rare and unjust laws? The President of the European Union?, The terrifying blonde Ursula? Our dear Ursula obeys her masters, because (they) pay her and her husband very well. Today, February 19, 2023, we have learned that the very

Goddess, queen of Europe, dictates that we will have to eat insects in some famous supermarkets in Spain, they already have the delicacy on the shelves, ready to consume. The infected television is ready to bomb the population, washing the face of the delicious worms and crickets that want to force us to eat. Insects are very harmful to humans, they contain a substance called chitin that is very dangerous, 'that,' is the real reason, so they want to introduce insects into our diet. But they say it is for the good of the planet!

For the good of the planet?!, in the sea there are trillions of fish, why can't we feed on fish? easy, fish are good for our health, and their plan, is, that we get very sick. I do not believe it! say the sleeping people, who do not bother to find out anything, nor do they question anything. It is hard to assume that the people who have to take care of you want to murder you and your loved ones. Many times, I feel envious of the sleeping abductees because they laugh more than me, they enjoy more than me, their minds have not changed! and their lives continue as before, many times, it is difficult for me to empathize with them, because their deep sleep drags us towards the path of destruction.

6

A narrow, gloomy path, prepared to live as slaves or robot slaves, which is not the same. Nanotechnology introduced treacherously, to all the inhabitants of the world, serves so that the tyrants who have always run the world, direct our brains. They did not have enough to manipulate our lives, they want to manage our mind!, our soul, the soul of our children!, they have introduced graphene oxide in the vaccines of the calendar, so that children are neuro modulated, from the cradle, and thus do with our little ones, the aberrations that they want. Sex, organs...,slavery..., and even now they intend to legalize pedophilia, terrifying?!, that is nothing, they want and wish with all their desire, to have fun, with the will of the people. For that they have bought and threatened governments 'just because,' they can also change the climate when they want. And they use that power to 'bribe' countries.

What an outrage! less than a hundred people dominating the entire world! Their job is to 'kill,' they are convinced, that they are doing a very great good for the planet. And why do not they start with themselves? Because what they want is for you to die. They are convinced that the planet is theirs! They want to enjoy it at will, have fun, because the world, according to them, belongs to them, and 'you' belong to them. Because if you do not do what they want, they will punish you without drinking water..., water? but if water is free, water belongs to everyone! 'not anymore.' In this country, the same government, empties the swamps and has destroyed three hundred dams, to what end? water will be a super luxury. A hot shower you will have to win, in what way? 'Injecting yourself with more poison.' For their abhorrent crimes to take place, they need to inject human beings for life.

Logically, if we all joined, we would end this criminal system in a few minutes. But at the moment that is not going to happen, right?, 'the political parties,' were created so that society is divided, one against another, and above all, entertained in defending our executioners, your executioners, they charge you for everything!, and you accept it!, resigned, (that is what there is), we are guilty for letting some criminals, are whipping us day after day. We are guilty of allowing injustice, we are guilty of not defending ourselves! and not defending others! we are guilty and guilty and more often guilty for allowing them absolutely everything! you are guilty! for not using your pride! for not respecting yourself! and for not respecting your children! and your children's children!

The world is a Paradise, it always has been, sea, rivers..., the world is an immense garden, so that human beings can be happy. Who burns the forests? who is burning everything? any guess..., 'them,' the same as always with their criminal activism. On YouTube we have a video, where a gentleman named Bill comes out telling people that there are millions of people left in the world, this element is the one that says that he saves your life with his spectacular vaccine! Tell you that he is forbidden to enter India, due to the thousands of dead and mutilated, (almost all children), that this man cheated with his vaccines, did you not know?, But everyone surrenders to his impressive wealth, not caring in the least about the dead that this lord has behind him, with his experiments. He wanders around the world like a peacock, bragging about his philanthropy, who's worse? Bill, or all those brown-nosing, slimy, and lacking people in morals and ethics, who laugh thanks to you?.

7

We also have our favorite comedian Elon! who with his silly face, never seems to have broken a plate. This handsome man, is the king of microchips, in a TV interview, two very excited journalists, wanted to know how he was going to introduce his chip to human beings, but he looked very uncomfortable, because he did not know how to explain it..., Until at the end he said, that the entrance had to be by vein!, the interviewers with bean's face, frowned, and taking a deep breath, they went on to ask another question. Mr. Elon loves robots... I am sure you have already noticed. Did you know that our stuffed animal Elon has nine children? These elitist sharks have many children, because their misdeeds are tradition in their families, for many years, hopefully! Some of his children, would continue with the plans of 'Dad,' when he died.

You see! they are not hiding! these heroes who sicken and kill treacherously, every day innocent people, they tell you to your face, how do I know? My question is for you, and I ask you, why do not you know? And... the director of the world health organization is not even a doctor! This gentleman cannot prescribe you a sad aspirin, as you can imagine 'Mr. Rouge,' because he is nothing more than a rogue, he intends to force all the people of the world to medicate whatever he wants, that is, following the orders of the supreme sharks.

The great Dr. Anthony, (specialized in immunology), and 'expert' in rheumatology and HIV, is the devil himself. All the people who more than thirty years ago, decided not to take their AIDS medication, saved their lives! but rest assured, that for Anthony it is no problem, to have killed so many people, because he has repeated it again! Politicians adore him, and they 'take care of him.' Total what else does it matter! if you already know that most people are not going to investigate anything about him, ah! by the way! it was the death doctor who advised to put on even masks! These are the visible faces, which we normally see in the press as not!

Our beloved Soros, is behind all conflicts, wielding his strings to his puppets, that there is a separatist movement? he is behind, that the movement is about racism? calm down, he is behind, that straight men are very bad?! he is behind. This sinister character is behind everything! The Instagram boy! very modest him, who wants to give the appearance of 'poor,' to give a mysterious image, before us, is also the protagonist of this great farce. The Sharks that hide behind the scenes, meet every year in Switzerland, since 1972, to plan what they are going to do with the world. The great 'Davos forum,' yes, there they are planning the policies of the countries. Electing the presidents or did you think that you have ever voted democratically? They elect the first-rank political presidents, yes, I was also disappointed, with such terrible news. They also plan wars, and of course, they provoke them, they decide which country is the good and which country is the bad, and they get it because they have bought all the press in the world. If any scientist discovers how to map the human brain, to be modulated, these sinister beings rub their hands, to be able to experiment with the population. And thus, be able to manipulate, murder, and abuse at will. They know they have the world in their hands, because they can buy everything, people, governments, politicians, singers, actors, and all the institutions they want.

They have also been dedicated to manipulating the weather since the eighties, I suppose you have heard that even in the desert, it snowed. On social networks there are videos showing how clouds are made, because as I said before, they are not hidden.

8

HAARP. Do you want to know what HAARP is? It is one, or some machines that serve to modify the weather, it works with electromagnetic outbreaks, which can cause earthquakes, tidal outbreaks, hurricanes and can even cause volcanoes, and guess who enjoys such a blessing?, Yes, them!, does it sound like volcanoes erupting, all over the world, in these last three years? Some earthquakes? very dangerous people with lethal weapons, and all this, they have managed, as I said before, 'with money.' In the history books, it is written what they want you to know, that is, they have been teaching the world, falsifying the past at will, for decades, minds molded and trained, by a gang of bullies, because that is what they are, phony bullies, that all they have is money.

Another hobby they have, first because that shows how ignorant they are, how simple they are, and also live in their crazy fantasy, which is, playing witches!, the bad thing about their schizophrenic hobby, is that they use the most defenseless beings on the planet, (children), they are part of their mental madness, every year hundreds of thousands of children disappear, they torture and kill them to satisfy their apocalyptic drunkenness, and all this they also achieve, 'paying.' With their money, they buy fear, and people's illusions. What are they afraid of this gang of ignoramuses? They are afraid that the inhabitants of the world will take off the raincoat of terror, which they have been making to measure for the consumer for centuries. A part of the world's population, you already know them! Now we know who they are, we know their names and surnames. Yes, they are mentally weak and sick people, hence they need to strangle with the hands of 'others,' the joy, strength, and spirit of all others, whom they describe as useless, useless eaters, sheep, they need to humiliate, insult, and kill, to feel important. Because deep down, they are nothing more than poor, bitter devils full of darkness. The day 'you' get rid of your fear, these criminals, who are nothing more than cowards who kill our children with treachery, will be naked primarily. Your money will not be able to buy the forgiveness and compassion of humanity.

Meanwhile, the weather planes, those small planes that leave a white trail, invade us every day, because it is not water vapor that they throw, they spread tons of heavy metals over our heads. Heavy metals are deadly for humans, apart from making us sick, with their poisonous trails, they cut the rains causing droughts, and elevated temperatures. When they are interested in lowering the temperature, they simply stop flying. Climate change is caused by the government, to carry out its Agenda of disease and destruction. To point out as guilty, the inhabitants of the planet of temperature change, is also a project of these macabre beings, called Elite Politicians. The consequence of their criminal acts, also cause the death and disappearance of many birds, are taking their toll on the ecosystem. Electromagnetic pollution is achieved thanks to the thousands of 5G antennas that were installed in the 2020 lockdown. Why did they hide them in the ground? why did they hide them by lining them so that they cannot be seen? Because when they open an antenna, in its inside, the words covid nineteen are written? the truth is that everything smells very bad, there is nothing good thought for us.

9

Mr. Klaus! says he is the executive president of the World Economic Forum, (forgive me) for not putting a photo of him. This character does not want us to die of old age, what he wants is to eliminate us when, according to him, 'we are already unnecessary,' because for this man, we are 'disposable' objects. He intends to take our lives, when he feels like it, because he says so! And his two balls! Aren't you laughing? Hahaha! But who is this element? who voted for it? I am going to think..., ah! Nobody! But this patient says of himself that he is 'God,' isn't it funny? laugh! All, laugh! All the presidents of the countries, he chooses them..., the president of Spain, signs up for all the misdeeds, which go through his head! The Davos forum!, That is where this worm goes to run the world!, he has made the seas, the mountains, he has made everything wonderful that is our planet!, and he has bought it together, with his friends, while they drink their glass of cognac!, 'but... who has sold them the world?' a world that is 'yours,' they have bought almost all the people we have around, to kill us! With the big lie of a virus or climate change that these psychopaths provoke.

What is going through their minds, the politicians who obey these crazy people?, The madmen give the order to burn the jungle, and these hollow heads do it! They also give the order to destroy the swamps, and these cretins do it! you do not realize ''you' brainless politician that you too, along with your whole family, are going to perish?

'You,' politician, will have nothing of what they have promised you, because you are garbage like them, and like garbage they are, like 'you' you will drown wrapped in your greed and your ignorance. These cowardly and insignificant beings, have the people of the planet controlled. They have bought us, because, someone has sold us, and who has sold us? Our 'Cowardice,' our carelessness, waiting for others to solve the problems of our home, our family and above all that of our children. We've put every child in the world in the hands of these sociopaths.

I did not know it..., you tell me, with a look of amazement!, but you tell me that you have to go, that you do not have time to talk to me, and you set course to continue with your miserable life, bowing your head, waiting for others to solve the problem, but the problem is you!, the big problem is 'you' who obey endlessly, everything that your rotten television says, you say that you do not watch television, but nevertheless you do and say everything that comes out of it! You tell me that yes, that everything is a hoax, but the next day you get vaccinated to go on a trip. A trip you can't enjoy, the pain is so severe that you have to go to the hospital! And you do not want to 'see' that the stroke you had was your fault, I warned you. But now you want to go eat at the restaurant, and you're happy because you have the passport of death. Not happy with that, you want to please others, and be part of the great mass accepted by television, because for this, you have been running to inject yourself with more poison. Now I can only tell you (may God have you in his glory) AMEN.

10

He calls himself the 'pope of Rome!' the friend of the poor! 'Representative of good.' Disguised in a luxurious robe, and a crucifix hanging on it, he manipulates and directs his great empire by directing the masses, 'Pope of Rome' who elected you? ah! The great 'column of smoke,' which depends on the color of the smoke, will let us know that you are the 'chosen one,' the saint who will free the world from its sins! thank goodness that we have 'you' Fran, who governs the Church. You tell the world what's right, and what's wrong, you know you're a phony and you can't hide it. But you like being there, and who are the white smokers? Oh! The Davos' Sharks. You have been told to pass on to humans, who are lucky to have two arms! One arm for one puncture, and the other arm for the next puncture. What about you? Fran? have you poked yourself? Oh! No, it is just that you, dear Fran, do not want to die.

You are not afraid of what you are doing Fran? you are not afraid to make people believe that you are God's command! Fran? Oh! I forgot, it is just that you, dear Fran, do not believe in God. You have disguised yourself in your huge cape, and like many people, you feel incredible adoration for yourself! Dear Fran.

There is a saying that says:
In order to do things wrong, you have to do them very well.
Only God can do miracles, do not trust the first one who appears,
He will abuse your desperation.

He will abuse your illness,
Of your poverty,
And he will even abuse your death.
Do not look for God in the wrong
place.
Do not look for him in the holy land.
Do not expect to find him, wearing a
tunic and sandals...

11

The Minister of Health of Spain has been campaigning in the Canary Islands, but in the middle of the walk, a citizen has rebuked her, asking her about the excess deaths between vaccination. The Minister smiles and says, thank you. This shameless lady in charge of the health of the Spaniards, (by the way she is not a doctor), uses her smile as a mask, her method of defense to be able to cover up how embarrassed she is, and she does it because her government advisors have recommended her to go crazy, if someone mentions the deaths from the punctures, Carol, go crazy! Have the

Canaries received the help they so badly need? No, but it does not matter, I am a lady, I want to be Mayor of La Palmas de Gran Canaria, just because, and because I deserve it. But you citizen are happy! Because Carol comes to 'change your future' for the better! When I am your mayor, your problems will be gone! Do not talk to me about a volcano! Because if you do, I am going to give you a cucumber on your face with my smile and... I'll disappear...hahaha!

The fault, citizen, is not mine, it is 'yours' for letting us politicians direct your life. You, citizen, only have to worry about the princess of the town, if she has put extensions in her hair..., if she has gone on a trip..., if she has divorced her last husband..., in short, the things that have always been important in your life. Also, citizen, you can discuss if your favorite team is the best, and not the neighbor! That he is a 'fool' to think that his football team will win. We also entertain you with a contest, where the famous participants, cannot sleep from the hunger that we make them go through! So that you get the idea of what your life will be like, and do not look at me, the politician, I only fulfill orders that I receive from my friends, the *carajilleros* of the Davos Forum.

When you go shopping for citizen clothes, make sure It is the trendy dress or pants! Because that way, if I see you, I'll know you're trained. In this way, the great Mass. will also accept you If you go to the city cinema, or if you prefer Netflix, you can enjoy the films and series that our masters, the *carajilleros* of Davos, have prepared for you to accept and normalize all the barbarities they intend, and that we politicians will oblige you to do with pleasure.

Because that is what we're here for, to support you when you pay your taxes, to help you if you ever want to change your sex, yes, you, a citizen, can change your name whenever you feel like it. If you are a man, immediately run to the civil registry. To choose the woman's name that you like the most. And if you are a woman, take off the heels that force you to wear, and choose the male name you like best. Oh! You can only change from male to female, and female to male! But... we hadn't met, that there is an infinite variety of genders? We politicians have forced in schools that there are more than two genders! What have we done wrong? You only have two 'options,' it cannot be.

Where will we get more variety of genders? Neither we nor our hundreds of advisors know how we are going to manage, wait... that is it! We will convince the youth that they feel like fish, dogs, cats, etcetera. And so, with so much mental trouble, and after a great deal of propaganda, people will be afraid to say that there are only two genders. And we will punish those who do not want to go through the tube, in this way, we will sow more terror.

12

Terror is what they want you to feel, you have no right, to feel hatred for anything or anyone. 'Hate' is an emotion that is in us, and that we should be free, whether we want to use it or not. Feeling hatred is not good, we already know, but it is a feeling that human beings have by nature, and therefore, no one can take it away from you. You have not realized that you cannot love either? Now, the fashion is that you only have sex without any feeling, and if it is with several people better! Because on television they make you understand it, and so they advertise it (continuously). Do you realize that you can only feel fear? fear of an illness, fear of a hurricane, fear of one more fine, fear of aliens! Dear citizen, 'we want you terrified,' and if for this, we have to tell you, that the UFO has come to control the world, do not hesitate! we will do it! Now it turns out that the aliens are here, and oh! coincidentally, they have met directly, with the president of the United States! Because everything happens there, in the United States! it would be scandalous, if someone who comes from another planet, meet you! or with a friend of yours! Well, no, they meet directly with the president..., It is just that we... we do not have as much category as him. They are preparing the way for you to love no one, and slowly lose the ability to love. If you feel love, it means that you can create and procreate. 'The owners of the world,' that is what they call themselves, they do not want you to have children. Only they can have offspring, it is a decision that they have made, on one of those boring afternoons that the bar has. And between drinks, and laughs! They decide that the children will no longer be delivered by 'women.' And voila... we will launch a great campaign so that the 'woman' is (hated) by the man. Feminism Fatalism! we create an aggressive movement, where the woman is always the victim! where the heterosexual man will be persecuted and blamed for everything that happens to the 'woman.' And for this we have the official media, sold for a handful of coins, to these old suckers, of the Davos forum. The mass will follow the Feminazi dictatorship because anyone who dares to think differently will be repudiated and removed from society. In this way, we get that the 'man' without realizing it, decides to remove the woman from her environment, if he wants to have sex, he has premises where he will find 'upon payment' the services he wants. The important thing is to separate men and women as soon as possible. These insane people try to manufacture 'children' artificially, will they succeed? They are rubbing their hands happily! thinking they are God. But there is only one God, and God will set all humankind against them, hence their perfection. God lives in each one of you, you will provide him with the strength he needs, you will be his tool, you will get up because he wants it that way, and you, all together, will be saved. For you are in God, and God is in you.

13

At this time, we are already starting to receive agricultural products from other countries, the policy of the 2030 Agenda is still on course, but for this, three years have been spent on destroying the agricultural industry. Workers in the sector have been warning for months about what is happening. But Spanish society, turns a blind eye, and shows not the slightest interest, in such a fundamental problem. They want to continue with their lives, totally 'oblivious' to such misfortune. Why are you going to worry, dear citizen? you yourself say, that you do not mind buying food from other countries, and you say it with all the brazenness and indecency! I wonder, really, you, citizen, deserve that someone fights so that you continue to swim on the sofa of your house, that someone fights so that you, citizen, continue with your miserable and disgusting life? I will answer you; No, no and a thousand times No! What angers me the most, damn 'citizen,' is that you believe that you are the Good! you repeat with your mouth full! that the good will win the Evil! Who is worse? the demon that wants to kill you? or You, who let them humiliate you repeatedly, knowing that they want to eliminate you, and allowing them to do the same with the people you love? 'No,' 'you,' citizen, you are not the Good. Good people! on social networks, there are videos where it is shown, how the fish are poisoned, before being sold, these images are visible to everyone, ah! I forgot, 'you do not care,' it is that You, are the 'good,' of this society. Also, and in view of everyone, there are images, where it is shown, that livestock in Spain is disappearing. And they tell you in great detail! but you do not know anything! because you have more important things to do. And let us not say about the three hundred swamps they have destroyed! It is okay, you, when the elections come, will put on your best clothes, to go and vote for your executioners! So, I have no choice but to tell you that 'you,' you are the damn problem! Your indifference, your ignorance, and your laziness are the passport of these tyrants! who are destroying the Country! You walk through life, as if everyone owed you something!, you feel so little, that you need some politicians to organize your life!, you need to be told what you have to eat, the medicine you have to take, when, and how you have to travel, and what pet you can have. Although you have accepted and very assumed, that these characters steal all the money they want. But poor of your neighbor! if you find out, that he is collecting an aid or a pension! because you will crucify him! Do not allow your neighbor to collect state aid, because you only give permission to your executioners, to be robbed! Do you still think you are the good? Do you still accept and approve that politicians continue to plunder and destroy the country? Do you still think that others deserve the dictatorship that you are crying out for? And you still think that you have to vote for a politician, for the simple reason that he has never governed!?, Knowing, in the depths of your being, what is another scammer?

14

For many years, I had a tremendous admiration for King Philip. I have always thought that the King would take care of the rights of all Spaniards. And realizing that all that, it was just an illusion of mine, has been very frustrating, and like me, many Spaniards, we had confidence in him. In these last three years, we said among ourselves, excited; Calm down! We have our King! Sure, he will do something for us! But the days and months passed, without any reaction. He could not accept, that he made all Spaniards believe, that he had given the famous injectable to his daughters.

And even he himself, too, had put on such a noble potion. In this way, many parents went to the vaccination centers to hand over their little ones to the dictatorial poke. The positive part of such disappointment is that we already know who he is, and whose side he is on. What good is a King? Is he to give prizes? For me, betrayal is the worst. May God forgive him because I..., The politicians of the first row, say that they have also injected themselves..., But none, in these three years, has died, nor have they fallen ill. A Spanish doctor says that they have not injected the potion. The images of them on television have deceived the entire population. Many of us already imagined it, 'placebo,' the lots are marked, some contain the fashionable concoction, and others contain saline water, because they are intended for the same people, who impose vaccination. According to them, vaccination without obligation, while a politician, lover of anchovies, says that people who do not want to be inoculated, be forced to do so, by 'the civilian' or by the 'military.' Yes, applauded by the crowd! Other politicians receive enormous benefits, thanks to vaccines, which they do not want to get themselves. The profits are so great that their greed prevents them from seeing the crimes they are committing. Despair makes many people have faith in the famous Nuremberg trials, which were also a huge hoax. In reality, they only judged and sentenced a little more than twenty people. That war lasted between 1945 and 1949, also caused by the same families, who have, according to them, 'bought the world.' Yes, the people who plan our future, including our death, are the descendants of the 'holocaust' criminals of the past. These criminals were educated to do evil, and now they are educating their children to torture ours. Evil is not only born, but also 'done.' We live in the lie they fabricate for us. They have turned our world, into a dunghill, into a Hell. And no, they are not the elite, they are just petty criminals with money.

15

The people who must teach our children, in schools, receive Orders, what orders? the orders to keep the children with the mask, 'well put,' to sanitize our children's hands, to have them completely separated, all the hours of 'their' working day. And they comply with the aberrant measures that have been entrusted to them. 'The torture.' The children are forced to attend school, threatening the parents with custody. Compassion does not exist in the Covid religion. Teachers, who try, without any success, to free the little ones from such an aberration, are quickly pointed out and crucified, sending them home, making them disappear, from such a monstrous school scenario. They do not question for a moment, because the disease attacks children from the age of six, and not before. Fear 'their fear' is the punishment that children receive day after day, also enduring the stupidity of their parents, who forget that their children need and must breathe. But fear! fear! is the one that rules everywhere. Fear is the only one that has the right to enter your house, your life..., and the one who is not afraid will be pointed out by the crowd. The children have been brutally tortured, by the imbecility of the adults, who do not question themselves, absolutely nothing. Without a doubt, the great heroes who have endured, and continue to endure such torture, without being able to DEFEND THEMSELVES, damn it! are the Children! God is weeping for them, for you have forsaken them! Blessed are our little ones, our young people, for to them belong the kingdom of God. God will gather and heal your son, because you yourselves, parents, have given them to the devil himself, you have given their souls to evil. You 'parents,' you are only interested in the acceptance of stupid people! and how stupid you are! You are singing towards the mouth of the wolf, accepting the mark of the beast! God stays, with the pieces that are left of your children, to be able to put them back together. God receives, with open arms, the innocence of your children! Since nothing and no one can ever steal them.

16

A six-year-old girl in Spain is being denied treatment to cure a tumor in her head. Because they say it is too expensive. And of course, you have to obey the orders, which politicians send. The doctors do not take to the streets to protest, in the face of tremendous criminal injustice. A six-year-old girl has been sentenced to death, and here she does not even protest. In the gatherings of the silly box, they do not discuss anything either. They also obey orders, and if such a terrible fate is denounced, it will be in vain. Because criminals design laws. Everyone follows orders! The Hippocratic oath that the doctors took, they have it unused. A few days ago, a child died of peritonitis, after having gone to the hospital three times. But the fact that people die for not being taken care of is already being normalized. Nothing happens, people will soon forget this tragedy, because if you tell someone about the problem we have in health, justice, food, and long etcetera, they all answer the same!: 'well, but we also have to live, do not we?,' but they do not understand, that someone will have to provide them, the life they are living..., this life! That what you are living is over...! They're telling you! Dumbass! and you roam and roam, that you want to continue with your life! and you are able to do so! to advise me, that I do the same as you! What are you afraid of? Of going to the dungeon? Oh! Yes, I forgot, in the dungeons there is no television, no hot showers, no sofa to put your ass in! sorry! they will not give you beer either! But... they are preparing the world, (including yours)! Where you will not have any of that. Because they have planned to take everything from you! And your family and your children are also included...! I know you feel, that something around you is not going well, after three years and a few deaths, between your friends and your family, now you know that something is not working. But... deep down, you wait and believe that you have the right! To have someone hurting themselves for you! While you're enjoying your pathetic life! You think that people who have not gone to university are wrong, that they are conspiranoids, anti-establishment, who want to attract attention. You look over their shoulders, even knowing that they haven't gotten sick in all that time. But you demand that they put the evidence on the table, without thinking for a moment, that your dear television is the one that does not provide any evidence. The lies of those worthless, which appear on your TV, only show that they are bought, by whom? by the people who say they love you, and will take care of you, if you give them your vote. In the meantime, you close your eyes and your mouth, in the face of the attempted murder of a six-year-old girl, who they do not want to cure, with the excuse that it is very expensive to save her. But nothing happens, if your children and your family are healthy, so that you can worry about the little one. What you want is to get on with your life, without anything or anyone bothering you. You know that in the supermarket, they sell insects, and it is funny, you're excited to record a video, cooking worms, for everyone to see, how nutritious they are, because an expert 'worthless' has said it, which is on your television screen! You do not suspect that the same 'expert' knows about viruses, the weather, wars...? really, does not light a bulb in your head? With such a terrible joke!

17

Neighborhood, the leaders have decided that humanity must be locked up within a fifteen-minute walk. And with the excuse of climate change, they can only go by public transport or scooter. Because the rich from now on, and because they feel like it, will be the only ones who can drive freely around the world. This is the world they are preparing, for all human beings. Oh, they also want you to buy three pieces of clothing per person per year. Because they have decided it. There will also be no lack of new proteins in your food! made up of delicious insects, which we can only eat, the amount they tell us for our own good! For this hell they are preparing to work..., who do they need? well, the police who protect them! 'yes' the same police as three years ago, pounced on the people who pay them, to force them to cover their nose and mouth. Blessed images, which exist to verify, how cowards they are, if you look for them, you will find them. Knock... knock..., is there any police officer there? Yes, you! Tell me; why do you beat the baker? why do you beat the boy, who works in the clothing store? why do you beat the people? Do not put on that face of not knowing anything!, tell me; why do you beat your brothers?! Why do dictatorships exist? Because traitors like you police, you protect criminals!, who abuse and torture the people! 'Your people!' But... you carry out orders! Are you laughing, do you want to stop reading...?, You like to be looked at with fear....you are waiting for someone to fail a little, to be able to hit them...,You like to put fines on innocent people..., You like to feel that you have the power!, to leave a family with children on the street...,You like to see how people give you the ball..., You like to insult and hit, hit and insult your brothers, because that makes you feel good! You know who to provoke, and then punish with armor, that your criminal bosses have put on you! because you, police, are the good guy. Your family, it is the people..., your friends are the people... And as a people who are your family and friends, they will also perish! Because you, you are preparing the way for your children! and your children's children! to be shot, by the same criminals that you, police, are protecting now. Oh! I forgot, 'you fulfill orders.' Remember police, there will be no hunger if you do not want to. There will be no injustice if you do not want to. Evil exists, because you police, you exist... All dictatorships exist because the security forces of the state protect these criminals.

18

So, you police officer, you protect evil, you take care that your 'executioners,' and the 'executioners' of humanity, are covered by your care. The army! are the ones who spread all the poison, with their weather planes, without thinking that they also live on the planet. Oh! I forgot! You are also fulfilling orders. Tell me... when you get off the plane, do you go somewhere in particular? Do you come back to recharge? How does it work? I feel a tremendous curiosity for you, you do it for...? Oh! Yes, what stupidity that I just said, 'you do it for money,' now you take helicopters! it does not matter that it is so brazen! it does not matter that people know it! because you are protected, by the electoral criminals. Who is in charge of burning the forests...? Do you take turns? the one who throws poison, also works in summer with the forests...? Do you have dates before you start? Do you take a small bottle of water, in case you are thirsty? Is the water you drink contaminated... or is your water bottle healthy? Do you charge a plus for nightlife? Tell me..., tell me..., is that you are really interesting people. Do you only know how to drive? Do you have any hobbies? Another question! Do you 'think'?... Ah! forgive my daring... you are fulfilling orders!). You can't think and follow orders at the same time... forgive me. Gentleman... Gentleman... these are the words you have been taught to say? Now I understand why you do not use your brain..., because if you use your head to think... you will realize how stupid you are. Bye! Gentleman.

That you are wondering, police officer and soldier, who am I? You have said it! because I AM. Another question? Are you friends with the intelligence services? Do you get along well? Forgive me for asking so much, but seriously, are you colleagues? Or... Do you work separately? I've seen many films, but you are undoubtedly the best! I AM your audience. You must be grateful! Because you have a job for life..., you have passed the exam without just studying, tell me: how is the control that you have passed? Very easy! but because in your book, there are only the words 'gentleman' and 'I do orders?' That is a trap hahaha, you approve only using your muscles, but why do you want so many muscles? If to arrest a teenager, you go at least ten police officers! Do you also call teenagers gentlemen? It is (curious.) Soldiers and police officers, are you willing to eat worms? Crickets? Cockroaches? Oh! It is true! You are just following orders.

Index